T0392281

REV. JOHN H. GIBSON

PREPARING
FOR THE
RAPTURE

WESTBOW
PRESS®
A DIVISION OF THOMAS NELSON
& ZONDERVAN

WestBow Press books may be ordered through booksellers or by contacting:

WestBow Press
A Division of Thomas Nelson & Zondervan
1663 Liberty Drive
Bloomington, IN 47403
www.westbowpress.com
844-714-3454

All Bible Scriptures are taken from King James
version of the Bible, public domain.

ISBN: 979-8-3850-3384-3 (sc)
ISBN: 979-8-3850-3385-0 (hc)
ISBN: 979-8-3850-3386-7 (e)

Library of Congress Control Number: 2024919860

Print information available on the last page.

WestBow Press rev. date: 11/15/2024

INTRODUCTION

On March 10, 1981, I was called by God to gather His people together for the rapture of His church. Though it took forty-three years to do this, I had to be prepared by Him and wait for Him before I could do it. He told me that when the time came, He would appear again to me and guide me through the whole process. You see, He waited until the time was right and has shown me everything that was going on in His churches and needed to be corrected for it to be raptured up. It took the entire forty-three years to show me all that is not being done right and all the sins of the leaders and the people, and to tell them what needs to be changed. Everything in this book will be backed up by scriptures from the Bible to show you that it is coming directly from God and not me. If the rapture comes today, the church will not be ready, and I hope to show you that in this book. I know that many of us truly love the Lord, but are we truly ready for His coming? The answer is no, and I hope to show this to all of us.

The answer will be revealed as we go through and see that God has shown us the way that we should serve Him. We feel that we are serving God by going to church on Sunday, that God hears all our prayers, and that we are doing all the right things that are pleasing in His sight. But we will see that nothing we are doing is acceptable to a holy God. Take heed to this scripture as it is written in 1 Corinthians 10:12: *"Wherefore let him that thinketh he standeth take heed lest he fall."*

A large number of you will feel offended by this book, and a few will receive it and make a change for the better. For the Lord has already warned me of what kind of people He is sending me to preach to. Look in Ezekiel 2:3–7.

> *And he said unto me, Son of man, I send thee to the children of Israel, to a rebellious nation that hath rebelled against me: they and their fathers have transgressed against me, even unto this very day. For they are impudent children and stiffhearted. I do send thee unto them; and thou shall say unto them, Thus saith the Lord GOD. And they, whether they will hear, or whether they will forbear, (for they are a rebellious house,) yet shall know that there hath been a prophet among them. And thou, son of man, be not afraid of them, neither be afraid of their words, though briers and thorns be with thee, and thou dost dwell among scorpions: be not afraid of their words, nor be dismayed at their looks, though they be a rebellious house, And thou shalt speak my words unto them, whether they will hear, or whether they will forbear: for they are most rebellious.*

So, I know what kind of people the Lord is sending me out to speak to. And I realize what He meant when He said that He has to close their eyes, ears, and hearts. Look in Isaiah 6:8–11.

> *Also I heard the voice of the Lord, saying, Whom shall I send, and who will go for us? Then said I, Here am I, send me. And he said, Go, and tell this people, Hear indeed, but understand not; and see ye indeed, but perceive not. Make the heart of this people fat,*

and make their ears heavy, and shut their eyes; lest
they see with their eyes, and hear with their ears, and
understand with their heart, and convert, and be
healed. Then said I, Lord, how long? And he answered,
Until the cities be wasted without inhabitant, and the
houses without man, and the land be utterly desolate.

That is until the Rapture comes, and total destruction is here. This is your final warning to make sure that you are ready. Let us not be too quick to judge, but let us keep an open mind and listen to what this book is telling us.

Now, I ask that you listen to the writings of this book, for it is for your good and not for your hurt. Truly, I was sent to do this for your sake. Look at John 13:20. *"Verily, verily, I say unto you, He that receiveth whomsoever I send receiveth me; and he that receiveth me receiveth him that sent me."* These are the words of the Lord Jesus Himself, and for sure, He has sent me to write this book. Look now at Hebrews 13:7 and 17.

Remember them which have the rule over you, who have
spoken unto you the word of God; whose faith follow,
considering the end of their conversation … Obey them
that have rule over you and submit yourselves: for they
watch for your souls, as they that must give account,
that they may do it with joy, and not with grief: for
that is unprofitable for you.

So, yes, I have been sent to have rule over you; I watch out for your souls and must give account to the Lord. Get ready for a lively awakening.

HOW TO GET READY
FOR THE RAPTURE
SEEKING AND FINDING GOD

We all say that we love the Lord and want to do the things that are righteous in His sight. But we don't know how to seek Him. *"And ye shall seek me, and find me, when ye shall search for me with all your heart"* (Jeremiah 29:13). You know nothing about God or what He expects of you but what you hear from preachers who were not called. The time has come that the Lord spoke of in Amos 8:11–13.

> *Behold, the days come, saith the Lord God, that I will send a famine in the land, not a famine of bread, nor a thirst for water, but of hearing the words of the LORD. And they shall wander from sea to sea, and from the north even to the east, they shall run to and fro to seek the word of the LORD and shall not find it. In that day shall the fair virgins and young men faint for thirst.*

And you are able to check them out in scriptures as did the people in Berea. Look at Acts 17:10–11.

> *And the brethren immediately sent Paul and Silas by night unto Berea: who coming thither went into the synagogue of the Jews. These were more noble than*

1

> *those in Thessalonica, in that they received the word*
> *with all readiness of mind, and searched the scriptures*
> *daily, whether those things were so.*

Therefore, you must receive the word with all readiness and search the scriptures daily to make sure what you heard was the truth. In this book, we are going to talk about false teachers and how to seek the Lord.

Now, here is the first thing you must do to seek and find God: eat (read) the word and eat it daily. The Lord has instructed me that I should not teach anyone who is not reading the word daily. And those that I do teach, when they witness to anyone, the first thing they advise them to do is to read their word daily. As a matter of fact, three times a day, because when you read the word, you are spending time (worshiping) with the Lord; and pray also. Look at Psalm 55:16–17.

> *As for me, I will call upon God; and the Lord shall save*
> *me. Evening, and morning, and at noon, will I pray,*
> *and cry aloud; and he shall hear my voice.*

Even when we advise people to read the word, they don't, and if they do, they don't do it the way that they are told. When the Lord called me, He told me to read the word from Genesis to Revelation and, when I finished, to start over and do it the same way until He came. Don't try to figure it out on your own because, every time you read it, the Holy Spirit will begin revealing it to you. So, every time you read the word through, more and more will be revealed to you by the Holy Spirit. We will speak more about the Holy Spirit later in this book.

By reading the word, you will no longer be simple but will become wise and have your soul converted. Look at Psalm 19:7, which says, *"The law of the Lord is perfect, converting the soul; The testimony of the Lord is sure, making wise the simple."* Because *"thy word is a lamp unto my feet, and a light unto my path"* (Psalm 119:105). In order to become wise, you first need wisdom. And if you lack wisdom, you can ask God and He will certainly give it to you. Look at James 1:5–8.

> *If any of you lack wisdom, let him ask of God, that giveth to all men liberally, and upbraideth not, and it shall be given him. But let him ask in faith, nothing wavering. For he that wavereth is like a wave of the sea driven with the wind and tossed. For let not that man think that he shall receive anything of the Lord. A double minded man is unstable in all his ways.*

So when you pray and ask God for anything, you must ask in faith and not doubt. All things you ask in prayer, by believing, you shall receive (Matthew 21:22).

The next thing we must do is pray. When we pray, we communicate with God on a personal level, with you talking with God and with Him answering you. Look at Luke 18:1, which says *"that men ought always to pray, and not to faint."* And now look at James 5:16b: *"The effectual fervent prayer of a righteous man availeth much."*

But you can only pray and have your prayer heard and answered if you have received the Holy Spirit and you are righteous. Look at John 9:31: *"Now we know that God heareth not sinners; but if any* man be a worshipper of God, and doeth his will, him he heareth." Look also at Romans 8:26–27.

> Likewise, the Spirit also helpeth our infirmities; for we know not what we should pray for as we ought; but the Spirit itself maketh intercession for us with groaning which cannot be uttered. And he that searches the hearts knoweth what is the mind of the Spirit, because he maketh intercession for the saints according to the will of God.

And now, here is the only way you can receive the Holy Spirit, and He will be with you forever. You cannot catch the Holy Spirit over and over again. He is given by the Father once and forever. Look at John 14:15–18:

> If you love me, keep my commandments. And I will pray the Father, and he shall give you another Comforter, that he may abide with you forever. Even the Spirit of truth; whom the world cannot receive, because it seeth him not, neither knoweth him; but ye know him; for he dwelleth with you and shall be in you. I will not leave you comfortless; I will come to you.

And please remember this. If you have the Holy Spirit, then you belong to the Lord Jesus Christ. Look at Romans 8:9: "But ye are not in the flesh, but in the Spirit, if so be that the Spirit of God dwell in you. Now if any man have not the Spirit of Christ, he is none of his."

Now, you have seen what you need in order to seek the Lord

God. You must seek Him with your whole heart. Look at Jeremiah 29:13. *"And ye shall seek me, and find me, when ye shall search for me with all your heart."* You must eat (read) His word and pray at least three times a day, the right way (from Genesis to Revelation). And you must keep His commandments so that the Lord Jesus Christ can pray to the Father and He will give you the Holy Spirit. Throughout all your years as a Christian, no one has told you these things or what you should do in order to seek and find God. Instead, they have told you that you should do nothing because you are already saved and don't have to do anything else. You have been so misled. But let me remind you that you will not one day just fall into heaven. You must work to accomplish this. Not to be saved but *because* you are saved.

So let us not continue to be simple but get wisdom. Pray and ask God, and He will surely give it to you, all that you need. Look at Proverbs 4:5–9:

> *Get wisdom, get understanding: forget it not; neither decline from the words of my mouth. Forsake her not, and she shall preserve thee: love her, and she shall keep thee. Wisdom is the principal thing; therefore get wisdom and with all thy getting get understanding. Exalt her, and she shall promote thee; she shall bring thee to honor, when thou dost embrace her. She shall give to thine head an ornament of grace; a crown of glory shall she deliver to thee.*

And again, if you do not have the Holy Spirit, you do not belong to the Lord Jesus Christ.

BEING READY FOR
THE RAPTURE

We all think that we are ready to enter God's kingdom when the rapture comes, but we are not. You must be ready, or you will not in any way enter. We must all walk in the Spirit and not in the flesh. And we can do this if we have received the Holy Spirit of God. Again, look at John 14:15–18.

> *If ye love me, keep my commandments. And I will pray the Father, and he shall give you another comforter, that he may abide with you for ever; even the Spirit of truth; whom the world cannot receive, because it seeth him not, neither knoweth him: but ye know him; for he dwelleth with you, and shall be in you. I will not leave you comfortless: I will come to you.*

When the Holy Spirit has come, He will guide you into all truth and will show you all things that will come (all God has promised you). Look at John 16:13–15.

> *Howbeit when he, the Spirit of truth, is come, he will guide you into all truth; for he shall not speak of himself; but whatsoever he shall hear, that shall he speak: and he will shew you things to come. He shall glorify me; for he shall receive of mine, and shall shew it unto you. All things that the Father hath are mine:*

therefore said I that he shall take of mine, and shall shew it unto you.

Then you will be able to walk in the Spirit and receive the benefits thereof. Look at Galatians 5:16–18.

This I say then, Walk in the Spirit, and ye shall not fulfill the lust of the flesh. For the flesh lusteth against the Spirit, and the Spirit against the flesh, and these are contrary the one to the other; so that ye cannot do the things that ye would. But if ye be led of the Spirit, you are not under the law.

Now if we do the works of the flesh, you will not inherit the kingdom of God. Look at Galatians 5:19–21.

Now the works of the flesh are manifest, which are these; Adultery, fornication, uncleanness, lasciviousness, Idolatry, witchcraft, hatred, variance, sedition, heresies, Envyings, murders, drunkenness, revellings, and such like: of the which I tell you before, as I have also told you in time past, that they which do such things shall not inherit the kingdom of God.

So let us receive the fruit of the Spirit, that we be not under the law but under grace. Look at Galatians 5:22–26.

But the fruit of the Spirit is love, joy, peace, long-suffering, gentleness, goodness, faith, meekness, temperance: against such there is no law. And they that are Christ's have crucified the flesh with the affections and lusts. If we live in the Spirit, let us also walk in the Spirit. Let us not be desirous of vain glory, provoking one another, envying one another.

So let us receive the Holy Spirit from the Father by the Lord Jesus and then walk in the Spirit. And let us not receive the wisdom that is earthly, sensual, devilish, that is not from above, but let us receive the wisdom that is from above. Look at James 3:14–17.

But if ye have bitter envying and strife in your hearts, glory not, and lie not against the truth. This wisdom descendeth not from above, but is earthly, sensual, devilish. For where envying and strife is, there is confusion and every evil work. But the wisdom that is from above is first pure, then peaceable, gentle, and easy to be intreated, full of mercy and good fruits, without partiality, and without hypocrisy.

Now, we see that if we walk in the Holy Spirit, we will no longer fulfill the lust of the flesh.

Let us look at how we will in no way have any condemnation if we continue to walk in the Spirit and not in the flesh. Let's look at Romans 8:1–17.

There is therefore now no condemnation to them which are in Christ Jesus, who walk not after the flesh, but after the Spirit. For the law of the Spirit of life in Christ Jesus hath made me free from the law of sin and death. For what the law could not do, in that it was weak through the flesh, God sending his own Son in

9

the likeness of sinful flesh, and for sin, condemned sin in the flesh: That the righteousness of the law might be fulfilled in us, who walk not after the flesh, but after the Spirit. For they that are after the flesh do mind the things of the flesh; but they that are after the Spirit the things of the Spirit. For to be carnally minded is death; but to be spiritually minded is life and peace. Because the carnal mind is enmity against God; for it is not subject to the law of God, neither indeed can be. So then they that are in the flesh cannot please God. But ye are not in the flesh, but in the Spirit, if so be that the Spirit of God dwell in you. Now if any man have not the Spirit of Christ, he is none of his. And if Christ be in you, the body is dead because of sin; but the Spirit is life because of righteousness. But if the Spirit of him that raised up Jesus from the dead dwell in you, he that raised up Christ from the dead shall also quicken your mortal bodies by his Spirit that dwelleth in you. Therefore, brethren, we are debtors, not to the flesh, to live after the flesh. For if we live after the flesh, ye shall die: but if ye through the Spirit do mortify the deeds of the body, ye shall live. For as many as are led by the Spirit of God, they are the sons of God. For ye have not received the Spirit of bondage again to fear; but have received the Spirit of adoption, whereby we cry, Abba Father. The Spirit itself bearers witness with our spirit, that we are the children of God. And if children, then heirs; heirs of God, and joint-heirs with Christ;

if so be that we suffer with him, that we may be also glorified together.

Now, let us look at all we have learned about the Holy Spirit. We learned that we cannot catch the Holy Spirit by hearing a gospel song, or by a feeling on Sunday and Him leaving us on Monday. We now know that the Spirit is given us of the Father, by the Lord Jesus Christ praying for us to receive Him, and that the Holy Spirit will be with us forever. We have also learned that if we have not the Spirit, we are not in Christ Jesus because in Jesus Christ, only are we righteous. We learned that we need the Holy Spirit in order to serve the Lord as we should, for He will teach us all truth, and all things to come. We learned that if we walk in the Spirit, we will not fulfill the lust of the flesh, for we know that the flesh works against the Spirit, and the Spirit against the flesh, and they are contrary to one another. We have learned what the works of the flesh are and what the gift of the Spirit is. So let us not continue to be ignorant; and do what it takes to receive the Holy Spirit. For we cannot walk as we should if we do not have the Holy Spirit. Nor will our prayers be heard, for it is the Spirit that takes our prayers to the Lord Jesus Christ and He intercedes with the Father for us. And in us will be no condemnation.

Now, we are going to look at Jeremiah chapter 7. This chapter was the final warning to Judah before it was destroyed by Babylon because they did not heed this warning. As did Israel when God sent Isaiah, Amos, Micah, and Hosea to warn them, and they did not listen and were destroyed by the Assyrians. And now, for us, there is a final warning if we don't listen to all that's given to us in this chapter of Jeremiah 7. If you don't, you will not be raptured up, but you will have to go through the great tribulation.

God has called me face-to-face and told me that He called me to gather His people together for the rapture of the church. So, by the guidance of the Holy Spirit, I will try to explain this chapter to you and hope you will listen and heed this warning. For if you do, you will be caught up to the Lord and will be with Him forevermore, even during the rapture. Now, we all think that we are prepared to be raptured up and are truly serving God. But here is what God says about that in Romans 3:10–12 and 18.

> *As it is written, There is none righteous, no, not one. There is none that understand, there is none that seeketh after God. They are all gone out of the way, they are together become unprofitable; there is none that doeth good, no, not one (10–12).*

> *There is no fear of God before their eyes(18). You must truly show God that you love him by keeping His commandments.*

John 14:15 says, *"If you love me, keep my commandments."* Read His word and pray three times a day and learn His commandments.

> *The word that came to Jeremiah from the LORD, saying. Stand in the gate of the LORD's house, and proclaim there this word, and say, Hear the word of the LORD, all ye of Judah, that enter in at these gates to worship the LORD. Thus saith the LORD of hosts,*

the God of Israel. Amend your ways and your doings, and I will cause you to dwell in this place. Trust ye not in lying words, saying, The temple of the LORD, The temple of the LORD, The temple of the LORD are these. For if ye throughly amend your ways and your doings; if ye throughly execute judgment between a man and his neighbor; if ye oppress not the stranger, the fatherless, and the widow, and shed not innocent blood in this place, neither walk after other gods to your hurt: Then will I cause you to dwell in this place, in the land that I gave to your fathers, for ever and ever. Behold, ye trust in lying words, that cannot profit. Will ye steal, murder, and commit adultery, and swear falsely, and burn incense unto Baal, and walk after other gods whom ye know not; And come and stand before me in this house, which is called by my name, and say, We are delivered to do all these abominations? Is this house, which is called by my name, become a den of robbers in your eyes? Behold, even I have seen it, saith the LORD. But go ye now unto my place which was in Shiloh, where I set my name at first, and see what I did to it for the wickedness of my people Israel. And now, because ye have done all these works, saith the LORD, and I spake unto you, rising up early and speaking, but ye heard not; and I called you, but ye answered not; Therefore will I do unto this house, which is called by my name, wherein ye trust, and unto the place which I gave to you and to your fathers, as I have done to Shiloh. And I will cast you out of my sight, as

I have cast out all your brethren, even the whole seed of Ephraim. Therefore pray not thou for this people, neither lift up cry nor prayer for them, neither make intercession to me; for I will not hear thee. Seest thou not what they do in the cities of Judah and in the streets of Jerusalem? The children gather wood, and the fathers kindle the fire, and the women knead their dough, to make cakes to the queen of heaven, and to pour out drink offerings unto other gods, that they may provoke me to anger. Do they provoke me to anger? saith the LORD: *do they not provoke themselves to the confusion of their own faces? Therefore thus saith the Lord* GOD; *Behold, mine anger and my fury shall be poured out upon this place, upon man, and upon beast, and upon the trees of the field, and upon the fruit of the ground; and it shall burn, and shall not be quenched. Thus saith the* LORD *of hosts, the God of Israel; Put your burnt offerings unto your sacrifices, and eat flesh. For I spake not unto your fathers, nor commanded them in the day that I brought them out of the land of Egypt, concerning burnt offerings or sacrifices: But this thing commanded I them, saying, Obey my voice, and I will be your God, and ye shall be my people: and walk ye in all the ways that I commanded you, that it may be well unto you.*

But they harkened not, nor inclined their ear, but walked in the counsels and in the imagination of their evil heart, and went backward, and not forward. Since the day that your fathers came forth out the land of Egypt unto this day I have even sent unto you my servants the prophets, daily rising up early and sending them: Yes they hearkened not unto me, nor inclined ears, but hardened their neck; they did worse than their fathers. Therefore thou shalt speak all these words unto them; but they will not hearken to thee; thou shalt also call unto them; but they will not answer thee. But thou shalt say unto them, This is a nation that obeyeth not the voice of the LORD their God, nor receiveth correction; truth is perished, and is cut off from their mouth. Cut off thine hair, O Jerusalem, and cast it away, and take up a lamentation on high places; for the LORD hath rejected and forsaken the generation of his wrath. (Jeremiah 7:1–30)

Chapter 7 of Jeremiah is where God has chosen to give a warning to the people of God first because judgment must first begin in the house of the Lord. "For the time is come that judgment must begin at the house of God; and if it first begin at us, what shall the end be of them that obey not the gospel of God?" (1 Peter 4:17)

And also in Ezekiel in chapter 8. God took Ezekiel through the temple (God's house) and showed him all the sins that were being committed within. Then, in chapter 9, He sent the Holy Spirit to seal (mark) those who were being righteous; and then He sent six more angels to destroy those who were not. Look in Ezekiel 9:1–7.

He cried also in mine ears with a loud voice, saying, cause them that have charge over the city to draw near, even every man with his destroying weapon in

15

his hand. And, behold, six men from the way of the higher gate, which lieth toward the north, and every man a slaughter weapon in his hand; and one man among them was clothed with linen, with a writer's inkhorn by his side: and they went in, and stood beside the brazen altar. And the glory of the God of Israel was gone up from the cherub, whereupon he was, to the threshold of the house. And he called to the man clothed with linen, which had the writer's inkhorn by his side; And the LORD said unto him, go through the midst of the city, through the midst of Jerusalem, and set a mark upon the foreheads of the men that sigh and that cry for all the abominations that be done in the midst thereof. And to the others he said in mine hearing. Go ye after him through the city, and smite; let not your eye spare, neither have ye pity: Slay utterly old and young, both maids, and little children, and women; but come not near any man upon whom is the mark; and begin at my sanctuary. Then they began at the ancient men which were before the house. And he said unto them, defile the house, and fill the courts with the slain; go ye forth. And they went forth, and slew in the city."

Notice in verse 6, *"Then they began at the ancient men which were before the house,"* that they began with the leaders of the churches, pastors, deacons, preachers, and teachers.

So now I'm going to give you all that the Lord has given me to explain what He is saying in this chapter. For He says in verse 1,

"The word came to Jeremiah from the Lord, saying." He has also given it to me. Because the judgment will begin with us first, He tells me in, verse 2, *"Stand in the gate of the Lord's house, and proclaim there this word, and say, Hear the word of the Lord, all ye of Judah, that enter in at these gates to worship the Lord."*

Now this word is first for the church and then also for everyone that hears and heeds to it, for God wants that none should perish but that all should come to repentance. Let us look at 2 Peter 3:9. *"The Lord is not slack concerning his promise, as some men count slackness; but is long-suffering to us-ward, not willing that any should perish, but all should come to repentance."* So let it be that everyone who reads this book takes heed to the warnings that it gives: *"Thus saith the Lord of hosts, the God of Israel, Amend your ways and your doings, and I will cause you to dwell in this place"* (Jeremiah 7:3). The LORD asks that you amend your ways and your doings, and here is why. Right now, your ways and your thoughts are not in line with GOD's. Look at Isaiah 55:7–9.

> *Let the wicked forsake his way, and the unrighteous man his thoughts; and let him return unto the LORD, and he will have mercy upon him; and to our God, for he will abundantly pardon. For my thoughts are not your thoughts, neither are your ways my ways, saith the LORD. For as the heavens are higher than the earth, so are my ways higher than your ways, and my thoughts than your thoughts.*

Now, here is how we amend our ways and make them more like God's ways. We can start by walking according to the way the

Bible teaches us to walk. Let's start first by looking at Ephesians 4:1–6.

> *I therefore, the prisoner of the Lord, beseech you that ye walk worthy of the vocation wherewith ye are called. With all lowliness and meekness with longsuffering, forbearing one another in love; Endeavoring to keep the unity of the Spirit in the bond of peace. There is one body, and one Spirit, even as ye are called in one hope of your calling; One Lord, one faith, one baptism, One God and Father of all, who is above all, and through all, and in you all.*

We have to walk worthy of our calling, with all long-suffering, being patient with one another and being united in the Holy Spirit with all lowliness and meekness, and help one another so that we all grow together.

Next, we are not to walk as other gentiles walk. Look at Ephesians 4:17–19.

> *This I say therefore, and testify in the Lord, that ye henceforth walk not as other gentiles walk, in the vanity of their minds. Having their understanding darkened, being alienated from the life of God through the ignorance that is in them, because of the blindness of their heart: 19. Who being past feeling have given themselves over unto lasciviousness, to work all uncleanness with greediness.*

You see, before the Lord Jesus Christ, we too walked according to the course of this world, according to the prince of the air (the devil), fulfilling the desires of the flesh and of the mind. But God, who loved us, made us alive again through Christ. Look at Ephesians 2:2–7.

Wherein in time past ye walked according to the course of this world, according to the prince of the power of the air, the Spirit that now worketh in the children of disobedience. Among whom also we all had our conversation in times past in the lusts of our flesh, fulfilling the desires of the flesh and of the mind; and were by nature the children of wrath, even as others.

But God, who is rich in mercy, for His great love wherewith He loved us, Even when we were dead in sins, hath quickened us together with Christ; And hath raised us up together, and made us to sit together in heavenly places in Christ Jesus: That in the ages to come He might shew the exceeding riches of His grace in His kindness toward us through Christ Jesus.

Even when we were dead in sins and walking as other gentiles, He has quickened (made us alive) us together with Christ and made us to sit together with Him in heavenly places.

We must also walk as children of light. Look at Ephesians 5:8–10.

For ye were sometimes darkness, but now are ye light in the Lord; walk as children of light: (For the fruit of the

Spirit is in all goodness and righteousness and truth;)
proving what is acceptable unto the Lord.

So let us not walk in darkness anymore as we used to. But let us walk circumspectly as wise and not as fools, and be filled with the Spirit. Look at Ephesians 5:15–18.

See then that ye walk circumspectly, not as fools, but as wise. Redeeming the time, because the days are evil. Wherefore be ye not unwise, but understanding what the will of the Lord is. And be not drunk with wine, wherein is excess; but be filled with the Spirit.

So let us not be unwise but understand what the will of the Lord is. Look at 1 Thessalonians 4:3–5.

For this is the will of God, even your sanctification, that ye should abstain from fornication. That every one of you should know how to possess his vessel in sanctification and honor; not in the lust of concupiscence, even as the Gentiles which know not God.

So let us be understanding of the will of God; and let us not walk in darkness or unwise anymore but walk in wisdom, and not as fools, but walk in the Spirit. Now we can walk in the Spirit if we are keeping God's commandments, and the Lord Jesus has prayed that God give Him (Holy Spirit) to us.

Now here is why we should amend our ways. Look at Jeremiah 7:5–7.

*For if ye throughly amend your ways and your doings; if
ye throughly execute judgment between a man and his
neighbor; If ye oppress not the stranger, the fatherless,
and the widow, and shed not innocent blood in this
place, neither walk after other gods to your hurt: Then
will I cause you to dwell in this place, in the land that
I gave to your fathers, for ever and ever.*

Now, if you want to dwell in the land that the Lord has given
you, which is His Kingdom, you must thoroughly amend your
ways and your doings. Thoroughly execute judgment between a
man and his neighbor. Oppress not the stranger (non-Christians),
fatherless (orphans), and widows and shed not innocent blood in
this place (cause others to sin) and do not walk after other gods.
Then will the Lord cause you to dwell in His kingdom. These are
things you do every day because you do not the things of God.
And as you will see, the Lord is not pleased with your efforts to
correct yourselves. Look at Proverb 3:5–6.

*Trust in the LORD with all thine heart; and lean
not unto thine own understanding. In all thy ways
acknowledge him, and He shall direct thy paths.*

Also, walk not after other gods to your hurt. You should only
walk after the true God and be obedient to Him and keep His
commandments.

Now let us look at Jeremiah 7:4 and 8.

> *Trust ye not in lying words, saying. The temple of the*
> *Lord, The temple of the Lord, The temple of the Lord,*
> *are these (4).*

You see that you listen to all the lying words of false prophets and believe everything they tell you. It ought not to be so. They are not sent by God and do not give you the things of the Bible. Now look at verse 8.

> *Behold, ye trust in lying words, that cannot profit (8).*

These lying words will not profit you, because how can you believe? Or how can you hear without a preacher? And how can they preach except they be sent? Look at Romans 10:14–15.

> *How then shall they call on him in whom they have not*
> *believed? and how shall they believe in him of whom*
> *they have not heard? and how shall they hear without*
> *a preacher? And how shall they preach, except they be*
> *sent? as it is written, How beautiful are the feet of them*
> *that preach the gospel of peace, and bring glad tidings*
> *of good things!"*

My dear brethren, not everyone who claims to be a preacher truly is. They have been sent by the devil to confuse you that you do not the things of God. This is why Jeremiah writes that in chapter 7, verse 8, Don't continue to let them deceive you. They are very real and like the devil their father, they are doing their jobs very well. Look at 2 Corinthians 11:13–15.

For such are false apostles, deceitful workers, transforming themselves into the apostles of Christ. And no marvel; for Satan himself is transformed into an angel of light. Therefore it is no great thing if his ministers also be transformed as ministers of righteousness; whose end shall be according to their works.

Now there have been false prophets among the people before us and they shall be also among us, and they will bring in destructive practices. And a lot of people will follow their evil ways. Look at 2 Peter 2:1–3.

But there were false prophets also among the people, even as there shall be false teachers among you, who privily shall bring in damnable heresies, even denying the Lord that bought them, and bring upon themselves swift destruction. And many shall follow their pernicious ways; by reason of whom the way of truth shall be evil spoken of. And through covetousness shall they with feigned words make merchandise of you: whose judgment now of a long time lingereth not, and their damnation slumbereth not.

Now God will punish them for what they have done to you, but it is up to you to put God's word in you so that you will not be deceived. And then you will know God's word and keep His commandments, for the Holy Spirit will reveal them to you. Now when the disciples ask the Lord Jesus of His return, the first thing

He told them was "take heed that no man deceive you." Look at Matthew 24:3-5.

> *And as he sat upon the mount of Olives, the disciples came unto him privately, saying. Tell us, when shall these things be? and what shall be the sign of thy coming, and of the end of the world? And Jesus answered and said unto them take heed that no man deceive you. For many shall come in my name, saying, I am Christ; and shall deceive many.*

Here is something else you should know about lying words. We are now living in the last times (hours) and days here on this earth. Notice all the evil, famines, and pestilences of these days. The Lord Jesus Christ spoke of these days in Matthew 24:28 when he showed His disciples what would be the signs of His coming. *"For wheresoever the carcass is, there will the eagles be gathered together"* (Matthew 24:28). When the famines and pestilences are coming more and more consistently, we know that the time is near for the rapture. Well, 1 John 2:18-21 warns us that this is because there will be many antichrists (false prophets) in these days. Now let's look at 1 John 2:18 and 19.

> *Little children, it is the last time: and as ye have heard that antichrist shall come, even now are there many antichrists; whereby we know that it is the last time. They went out from us, but they were not of us; for if they had been of us, they would no doubt have continued with us; but they went out, that they might be made manifest that they were not all of us.*

What John is saying in verse 19 is that they were part of us but have now chosen their own way, having a form of godliness but denying the power thereof. Look at 2 Timothy 3:4 and 5.

Traitors, heady, high-minded, lovers of pleasures more than lovers of God; Having a form of godliness but denying the power thereof: from such turn away.

These so say Christians love pleasures more than God. They also have a form of godliness, but deny the power thereof; and you are advised to turn away from them.

Now let us look at what the writers of the Bible say about these false prophets. I'm going to give you just a few of them. Let's look first at what Jeremiah says in Lamentations 2:14: *"Thy prophets have seen vain and foolish things for thee: and they have not discovered thine iniquity. to turn away thy captivity; but have seen for thee false burdens and causes for banishment."*

Now Jeremiah 14:14: *"Then the Lord said unto me, The prophets prophesy lies in my name: I sent them not, neither have I commanded them, neither spake unto them: they prophesy unto you a false vision and divination, and a thing of naught, and the deceit of their heart."*

Here are some warnings about these false prophets (antichrists):

- *"Beware of false prophets, which come to you in sheep's clothing, but inwardly they are ravening wolves"* (Matthew 7:15).
- *"And many false prophets shall rise, and shall deceive many"* (Matthew 24:11).

- *"For there shall arise false Christs, and false prophets, and shall shew great signs and wonders; insomuch that, if it were possible, they shall deceive the very elect"* (Matthew 24:24).

- *"For false Christs and false prophets shall rise, and shall shew signs and wonders, to seduce, if it were possible, even the elect"* (Mark 13:22).

And now 1 John 4:1: *"Beloved, believe not every spirit, but try the spirits whether they are of God: because many false prophets are gone out into the world."* They are here to seduce you and turn you away from God. So, beware because they are very serious about what they do.

In these last days or hours, the Lord is not blind to what is happening. But if you turn to Him and be obedient to His every word, He knows how to deliver the godly out of temptations, and to reserve the unjust unto the day of judgment to be punished. For in these days there shall be many false prophets.

Look at 2 Peter 2:1–3 and verse 9.

But there were false prophets also among the people, even as there shall be false teachers among you, who privily shall bring in damnable heresies, even denying the Lord that bought them, and bring upon themselves swift destruction. And many shall follow their pernicious ways; by reason of whom the way of truth shall be evil spoken of.

And through covetousness shall they with feigned words make merchandise of you; whose judgment now for a long time lingereth not, and their damnation slumbereth not. (2 Peter 2:1–3)

The Lord knoweth how to deliver the godly out of temptations, and to reserve the unjust unto the day of judgment to be punished. (2 Peter 2:9)

For the Holy Spirit speaks clearly about what should happen in the last days. Look in 1 Timothy 4:1 and 2.

Now the Spirit speaketh expressly, that in the latter times some shall depart from the faith, giving heed to seducing spirits, and doctrines of devils; Speaking lies in hypocrisy; having their conscience seared with a hot iron.

So let us not continue to listen to teachers that have not received the Holy Spirit and are not true followers of the Lord Jesus Christ.

Now we will see that even the Lord Jesus Christ Himself has condemned the false prophets, which are the pastors and teachers of these days. For the Lord calls them hypocrites. Look at Matthew 23:13–15.

But woe unto you, scribes and Pharisees, hypocrites! for ye shut up the kingdom of heaven against men; for ye neither go in yourselves, neither suffer ye them that are entering to go in. Woe unto you, scribes and Pharisees, hypocrites! for ye devour widows' houses, and for a pretense make long prayer; therefore, ye shall

27

receive the greater damnation. Woe unto you, scribes
and Pharisees, hypocrites! for ye compass sea and land
to make one proselyte, and when he is made, ye make
him twofold more the child of hell than yourselves.

You see how they take new converts that want to become Christians and double their chances of going to hell? This is very much the case of what's happening in the churches in these later days. The churches are not in any wise growing in these days. Look at 2 Timothy 3:7. *"Ever learning, and never able to come to the knowledge of the truth."*

The Lord continues His criticizing of these false prophets and false teachers. Here He begins with saying that they promote paying tithes and offerings but omit all the things they are to be concerned about. He also speaks about them appearing to be righteous but are really wolves in sheeps clothing, and discard the prophets that are sent by Him. Look at Matthew 23: 23–36.

Woe unto you, scribes and Pharisees, hypocrites! for
ye pay tithe of mint and anise and cumin, and have
omitted the weightier matters of the law, judgment,
mercy, and faith: these ought ye have done, and not to
leave the other undone. Ye blind guides, which strain
at a gnat, and swallow a camel. Woe unto you, scribes
and Pharisees, hypocrites! for ye make clean the outside
of the cup and of the platter, but within they are full
of extortion and excess. Thou blind Pharisee, cleanse
first that which is within the cup and platter, that
the outside of them may be clean also. Woe unto you,
scribes and Pharisees, hypocrites! for ye are like unto

whited sepulchers, which indeed appear beautiful outward, but are within full of dead men's bones, and of all uncleaness. Even so ye also outwardly appear righteous unto men, but within are full of hypocrisy and iniquity. Woe unto you, scribes and Pharisees, hypocrites! because ye build the tombs of the prophets, and garnish the sepulchers of the righteous, And say, if we had been in the days of our fathers, we would not have been partakers with them in the blood of the prophets. Wherefore ye be witnesses unto yourselves, that ye are the children of them which killed the prophets. Fill ye up then the measure of your fathers. Ye serpents, ye generation of vipers, how can ye escape the damnation of hell? Wherefore, behold, I send unto you prophets, and wise men, and scribes: and some of them ye shall kill and crucify; and some of them shall ye scourge in your synagogues, and persecute them from city to city: That upon you may come all the righteous blood shed upon the earth, from the blood of righteous Abel unto the blood of Zacharias son of Barachias, whom ye slew between the temple and the altar. Verily I say unto you, All these things shall come upon this generation."

Now all these examples were given so that you would know that there are many false prophets among you, and they will be here until the Lord comes for the rapture. So let us do what the Bible says in 1 John 4:1–3.

Beloved, believe not every spirit, but try the spirits whether they are of God: because many false prophets are gone out into the world. Hereby know ye the Spirit of God: Every spirit that confesseth that Jesus Christ is come in the flesh is of God: and every spirit that confesseth not that Jesus Christ is come in the flesh is not of God: and this is that spirit of antichrist, whereof ye have heard that it should come; and even already is it in the world.

Now let's see how these lying words that are given you do not line up with the Bible. You have been told to say things like "get thee behind me Satan," or "the devil is under your feet." Yet the Bible says you are not to dispute (fight) with the devil, where in your flesh of uncleanness, you despise government and speak evil of dignities. Whereas angels bring not accusation against them. Look at 2 Peter 2:10–14.

But chiefly them that walk after the flesh in the lust of uncleanness and despise government. Presumptuous are they, self-willed, they are not afraid to speak evil of dignities. Whereas angels, which are greater in power and might, bring not railing accusation against them before the Lord. But these, are natural brute beasts, made to be taken and destroyed, speak evil of the things that they understand not; and shall utterly perish in their own corruption; And shall receive the reward of unrighteousness, as they that count it pleasure to riot in the day times. Spots they are and blemishes, sporting themselves with their own deceiving while they feast

with you: having eyes full of adultery, and that cannot
cease from sin; beguiling unstable souls: an heart they
have exercised with covetous practices; cursed children.

Now look at Jude 1:8–10.

Likewise also these filthy dreamers defile the flesh,
despise dominion, and speak evil of dignities. Yet
Michael the archangel, when contending with the
devil he disputed about the body of Moses, durst not
bring against him a railing accusation, but said, The
Lord rebuke thee.

But these speak evil of those things which they
know not; but what they know naturally, as brute
beasts, in those things they corrupt themselves.

This is how you know that you should not go against the devil.
Because the archangel Michael, who is the great prince of the
children of God, did not bring up a railing accusation against him,
but said the Lord rebuke you (Satan). So now let us not continue
to trust in lying words, for they will truly lead us to disrespect the
Bible. And they cannot profit you. Look in Jeremiah 7:8. *"Behold,*
ye trust in lying words, that cannot profit."

Now we know that we should stay away from lying words and
false prophets because it is commanded of the Lord. When He
was asked of the disciples to show them of His return, His first
commandment was that they take heed that no man deceive them.
Look at Matthew 24:4 and 5.

And Jesus answered and said unto them, Take heed that no man deceive you. For many shall come in my name saying I am Christ; and shall deceive many.

And consider Jeremiah 7:9–11.

Will ye steal, murder, and commit adultery, and swear falsely, and burn incense unto Baal, and walk after other gods whom ye know not; And come and stand before me in this house, which is called by my name, and say, We are delivered to do all these abominations? Is this house, which is called by my name, become a den of robbers in your eyes? Behold, even I have seen it, saith the Lord.

Yes, you do steal, murder, and commit adultery, and swear falsely, and burn incense unto Baal, and walk after other gods whom you know not. In my forty-three years of ministering before God, I have seen it. And then you come and stand before the Lord in His house, which is called by His name and say, you are delivered to do these abominations. The Lord says, Behold even He has seen it. You see God sees all that is happening in His churches and does not miss a thing that is going on, because He knows everything about you.

Let's look at Psalms 139:1–12.

(To the chief Musician, A Psalm of David). O LORD, thou hast searched me, and known me. Thou knows my downsitting and mine uprising, thou understands

my thought afar off. Thou compasses my path and my lying down, and art acquainted with all my ways.

For there is not a word in my tongue, but, lo, O LORD, thou knows it altogether. Thou has beset me behind and before, and laid thine hand upon me. Such knowledge is too wonderful for me; it is high, I cannot attain unto it. Whither shall I go from thy spirit? or whither shall I flee from thy presence.

If I ascend up into heaven, thou art there: if I make my bed in hell, behold, thou art there. If I take the wings of the morning, and dwell in the uttermost parts of the sea; Even there shall thy hand lead me, and thy right hand shall hold me. If I say, Surely the darkness shall cover me; even the night shall be light about me. Yea, the darkness hideth not from thee; but the night shineth as the day: the darkness and the light are both alike to thee.

So now you see that everything you do, think, or say, the Lord knows it all. For an example of this, let's look at the thinking of these false prophets. Let's look at Micah 3:11: *"The heads thereof judge for reward, and the priests thereof teach for hire, and the prophets thereof divine for money: yet will they lean upon the Lord, and say, is not the Lord among us? none evil can come upon us."*

Now because God has seen all that you are doing and you refuse to return to Him, He issues a warning to all of you that do these things. Let's look at Jeremiah 7:12–15.

But go ye now unto my place which was in Shiloh, where I set my name at the first, and see what I did to it for the wickedness of my people Israel. And now because ye have done all these works, saith the LORD, and I spake unto you, rising up early and speaking, but ye heard not; and I called you, but ye answered not; Therefore will I do unto this house, which is called by my name, wherein ye trust, and unto the place which I gave to you and to your fathers, as I have done to Shiloh. And I will cast you out of my sight, as I have cast out all your brethren, even the whole seed of Ephraim.

Let us see what the Lord is saying here, as He issues this warning. Verse 12. Now look at Shiloh, where he sat up His first congregation when they entered the land He promised to give them. A promise made to Abraham, Isaac, and Jacob. Look at Joshua 18:1. *"And the whole congregation of the children of Israel assembled together at Shiloh, and set up the tabernacle of the congregation there. And the land was subdued before them."* And He promised them this in Deuteronomy 12:5 and 11.

But unto the place which the LORD your God shall choose out of all your tribes to put His name there, even unto his habitation shall ye seek, and whether thou shalt come (5).

Then there shall be a place which the LORD your God shall choose to cause his name to dwell there; thither shall ye bring all that I command you; your burnt

offerings and your sacrifices, your tithes, and the heave
offering of your hand, and all your choice vows which
ye vow unto the LORD (11).

So now you see that the first place that the LORD setup for His people to assemble was Shiloh, which He promised them back in Deuteronomy before it was set up, and it was where the people had their first congregation. Also, in Jeremiah 7:12, the LORD said, *"And see what I did to it (Shiloh) for the wickedness of my people Israel."*

Let's look at Psalms 78:60–64.

So that he forsook the tabernacle of Shiloh, the tent
which he placed among men; And delivered his
strength into captivity, and his glory into the enemy's
hand. He gave his people over also unto the sword; and
was wroth with his inheritance. The fire consumed
their young men; and their maidens were not given
to marriage. Their priests fell by the sword; and their
widows made no lamentation.

The LORD will do also the same to us if we continue to do all these wicked things and abominations. So let us not continue in our disobeying of His laws, statutes, commandments, and judgments.

Now let us look at Jeremiah 7:13–15.

And now, because ye have done all these works, saith
the LORD, and I spake unto you, rising up early and
speaking, but ye heard not; and I called you, but ye

answered not; Therefore will I do unto this house,
which is called by my name, wherein ye trust, unto the
place which I gave to you and to your fathers, as I have
done to Shiloh. And I will cast you out of my sight, as
I have cast out all your brethren, even the whole seed
of Ephraim.

First let us look at verse 13. *"Because ye have done all these*
works and I spake unto you, rising up early and speaking, but you
heard not; and I called you, but ye answered not." You see the LORD
woke me up early every morning, preparing me to write this book,
and preparing me to teach every Sunday morning, and He gives
me all that I have said to you. And He says that you heard not. He
says that He called you, but you answered not. Look at Jeremiah
7:25–27.

Since the day that your fathers came forth out of the
land of Egypt unto this day I have even sent unto you
all my servants the prophets, daily rising up early and
sending them; Yet they hearkened not unto me, nor
inclined their ear, but hardened their neck: they did
worse than their fathers. Therefore thou shalt speak
all these words unto them; but they will not hearken
to thee; thou shalt also call unto them; but they will
not answer thee.

It's been over forty-three years ago since the Lord has called
me to prepare His people for the rapture of the church. Many
times, He has awakened me very early in the morning making

me ready so that I can not only do my calling, but also fulfill His calling, giving me these scriptures in Romans 10:14–15.

> *How then shall they call on him in whom they have not believed? and how shall they believe in him of whom they have not heard? and how shall they hear without a preacher? And how shall they preach, except they be sent? as it is written, How beautiful are the feet of them that preach the gospel of peace, and bring glad tidings of good things.*

And again, the Lord has warned me that you will not listen to me, because you did not listen to Him, and that you are an impudent (hardheaded) and a rebellious house. Look at Ezekiel 3:7–11.

> *But the house of Israel will not hearken unto thee; for they will not hearken unto me; for all the house of Israel are impudent and hardhearted. Behold, I have made thy face strong against their faces, and thy forehead strong against their foreheads. As an adamant harder than flint have I made thy forehead; fear them not, neither be dismayed at their looks. though they be a rebellious house. Moreover He said unto me, Son of man, all my words that I shall speak unto thee receive in thine heart, and hear with thine ears. And go, get thee to them of the captivity, unto the children of thy people, and speak unto them, and tell them, Thus saith the Lord GOD; whether they will hear, or whether they will forbear.*

Now look at verses 14 and 15 of Jeremiah 7: *"Therefore will I do unto this house, which is called by my name, wherein ye trust, and unto the place which I gave to you and to your fathers, as I have done to Shiloh. And I will cast you out of my sight, as I have cast out all your brethren, even the whole seed of Ephraim."* God is saying, as He did to the whole tribe of Ephraim (Israel), He will do unto you and will destroy you. As they also were called by His name and trusted in it. They and their fathers, as He did to Shiloh, and He will cast you out of His sight. So, you must turn from your wicked ways and turn back to Him. God does not play favorites with anyone; He will reward you according to your doings. God said, He is tired of hearing you say, God wouldn't do that. When you say things like that, you are suppressing His word in unrighteousness. You must believe what He is saying in His word. Look at Romans 1:18–20.

> *For the wrath of God is revealed from heaven against all ungodliness and unrighteousness of men, who hold the truth in unrighteousness; Because that which may be known of God is manifest in them.*
>
> *For the invisible things of him from the creation of the world are clearly seen, being understood by the things that are made, even his eternal power and Godhead; so that they are without excuse.*

You see God will do to you as He did to Shiloh because it is written in His word. So, what He said will come to pass.

Now Jeremiah 7:16: *"Therefore pray not thou for this people, neither lift up cry nor prayer for them, neither make intercession to me: for I will not hear thee."* And He said, not only should I not pray for you, because He will not hear me, but He will not hear you when you pray in your time of troubles.

Look at Jeremiah 11:14: *"Therefore pray not thou for this people, neither lift up a cry or a prayer for them: for I will not hear them in the time that they cry unto me for their trouble."* The Lord also told me not to pray for you for your good. And when you fast, He will not hear your cry, or when you offer burnt offerings or oblations (your gifts), He will not accept them. Because you listen to your false preachers instead of Him. Look at Jeremiah 14:11–16.

> *Then said the LORD unto me, Pray not for this people for their good. When they fast, I will not hear their cry; and when they offer burnt offering and an oblation, I will not accept them; but I will consume them by the sword, and by the famine, and by the pestilence. Then said I, Ah, Lord God! behold, the prophets say unto them, Ye shall not see the sword, neither shall ye have famine; but I will give you assured peace in this place. Then the LORD said unto me, The prophets prophesy lies in my name; I sent them not, neither have I commanded them, neither spake unto them: they prophesy unto you a false vision and divination, and a thing of naught, and the deceit of their heart. Therefore thus saith the LORD concerning the prophets that prophesy in my name, and I sent them not, yet they say, Sword and famine shall not be in this land; By sword and famine shall those prophets be consumed. And the people to whom they prophesy shall be cast out in the streets of Jerusalem because of the famine and the*

sword; and they shall have none to bury them; them, their wives, nor their sons, nor their daughters; For I will pour their wickedness upon them.

Now look at Jeremiah 7:17–19.

Seest thou not what they do in the cities of Judah and in the streets of Jerusalem? The children gather wood, and the fathers kindle the fire, and the women knead their dough, to make cakes to the queen of heaven, and to pour out drink offerings unto other gods, that they may provoke me to anger. Do they provoke me to anger? saith the LORD; do they not provoke themselves to the confusion of their own faces?

Here we see that the people provoke the Lord to anger by preparing themselves, their children, their fathers, and their women to worship other gods besides the Lord. They believe that anything other than God is controlling their lives. Look at Ezekiel 8:6–9.

He said furthermore unto me. Son of man, seest thou what they do? even the great abominations that the house of Israel committeth here, that I should go far from my sanctuary? but turn thee yet again, and thou shalt see greater abominations. And he brought me to the door of the court; and when I looked, behold a hole in the wall. Then said he unto me, dig now in the wall; and when I had digged in the wall, behold a door. And he said unto me, Go in, and behold the wicked abominations that they do here.

The Lord also talks about the queen of heaven and other gods. The people do not serve God themselves, or their children, but follow other gods and wonder why their children do things that are not in line with the right things they should be doing. Let us look at Jeremiah 44:17–19 and verse 25.

But we will certainly do whatsoever thing that goeth forth out of our own mouth, to burn incense unto the queen of heaven, and to pour out drink offerings unto her, as we have done, we, and our fathers, our kings, and our princes, in the cities of Judah, and in the streets of Jerusalem; for then had we plenty of victuals, and were well, and saw no evil. But since we left off to burn incense to the queen of heaven, and to pour out drink offerings unto her, we have wanted all things, and have been consumed by the sword and by the famine. And when we burned incense to the queen of heaven, and poured out drink offerings unto her, did we make cakes to worship her, and poured drink offerings unto her, with our men? (17–19)

Thus saith the LORD of hosts, the God of Israel, saying; Ye and your wives have both spoken with your mouths, and fulfilled with your hand, saying, We will surely perform our vows that we have vowed, to burn incense to the queen of heaven, and to pour out drink offerings

unto her; ye will surely accomplish your vows, and
surely perform your vows. (25)

And now because you have made up your minds and have
put it in your hearts to do these things, the Lord has had Paul
write in 1 Corinthian 10:22 these words. *"Do we provoke the Lord*
to jealousy? are we stronger than he?" And that's why He asks in
Jeremiah 7:19. *"Do they provoke me to anger? saith the Lord: do*
they not provoke themselves to the confusion of their own faces?"
You see, you are not only provoking the Lord to anger, but also
bringing shame and destruction to yourselves by doing so. This
will only bring God's fury and anger upon them that do so. Let's
look at verse 20 of Jeremiah chapter 7. *"Behold thus saith the Lord*
God; mine anger and my fury shall be poured out upon this place,
upon man, and upon beast, and upon the trees of the field, and the
fruit of the ground; and it shall burn, and shall not be quenched."
Now let's look at Jeremiah 7:21–22.

> *Thus saith the LORD of hosts, the God of Israel; Put*
> *your burnt offerings unto your sacrifices, and eat flesh.*
> *For I spake not unto your fathers, nor commanded*
> *them in the day that I brought them out of Egypt,*
> *concerning burnt offerings or sacrifices.*

Now because you have chosen to seek other gods and bring
useless sacrifices, unwanted songs and prayers before the Lord,
here is what he says about that. First let us look at Isaiah 1:11–15.

> *To what purpose is the multitude of your sacrifices unto*
> *me? saith the LORD: I am full of the burnt offerings of*

rams, and the fat of fed beasts; and I delight not in the blood of bullocks, or of lambs, or of he goats. When ye come to appear before me, who hath required this at your hand, to tread my courts? Bring no more vain oblations; incense is an abomination unto me; the new moons and sabbaths, the calling of assemblies, I cannot away with; it is iniquity, even the solemn meeting. Your new moons and your appointed feasts my soul hateth; they are a trouble unto me; I am weary to bear them. And when ye spread forth your hands, I will hide mine eyes from you; yea, when ye make many prayers, I will not hear; your hands are full of blood.

The LORD says, He will not even hear your prayers. Read what He says in John 9:31. *"Now we know that God heareth not sinners: but if any be a worshiper of God, and doeth his will, him he heareth."* And He says further in Amos 5:21–23.

I hate, I despise your feast days, and I will not smell in your solemn assemblies. Though ye offer your meat offerings, I will not accept them: neither will I regard the peace offerings of your fat beasts. Take thou away from me the noise of thy songs; for I will not hear the melody of thy viols.

Jeremiah 7:23 says, *"But this thing commanded I them, saying, Obey my voice, and I will be your God, and ye shall be my people; and walk ye in all the ways that I have commanded you, that it may be well unto you."* Now look at Jeremiah 11:4 and 11:7.

Which I commanded your fathers in the day I brought them forth out of the land of Egypt, from the iron furnace, saying, Obey my voice, and do them according to all which I commanded you: so shall ye be my people, and I will be your God (4).

For I earnestly protested unto your fathers in the day I brought them up out of Egypt, even unto this day, rising early and protesting, saying, Obey my voice (7).

The Lord wants you to be obedient, He does not want your sacrifices. Look at Exodus 15:26 and 19:5.

And said, if thou wilt diligently hearken to the voice of the LORD thy God, and wilt do that which is right in his sight, and will give ear to his commandments, and keep all his statutes, I will put none of these diseases upon thee, which I have brought upon the Egyptians: for I am the LORD that healeth thee." (15:26)

"Now therefore, if ye will obey my voice indeed, and keep my covenant, then ye shall be a peculiar treasure unto me above all people: for all the earth is mine." Hear you not what the Lord said. If you obey His voice indeed, you shall be a peculiar (special) treasure unto Him. (19:5)

Jeremiah 7:24 says, "*But they hearkened not, nor inclined their ear, but walked in the counsels and in the imagination of their evil heart, and went backward, and not forward.*" You still say, even in these days that you will not listen to what the Lord has to say but are walking in the imagination of your hearts. And are going backward instead of going forward, and despising all that the Lord is saying. And you believe that no evil will come upon you.

Look at Jeremiah 23:17. *"They say still unto them that despise me. The Lord hath said, Ye shall have peace; and they say unto every one that walketh after the imagination of his own heart, No evil shall come upon you."* Please, stop listening to those teachers and preachers that God has not sent. For the Lord, even in these last days has sent unto you prophets to guide you in the way that you should walk. Look what the Lord says in Jeremiah 7:25–26.

> *Since the day that your fathers came forth out of the land of Egypt unto this day I have even sent unto you all my servants the prophets, daily rising up early and sending them: Yet they hearkened not unto me, nor inclined their ear, but hardened their neck: they did worse than their fathers.*

Look at Jeremiah 17:23. *"But they obeyed not, neither inclined their ear, but made their neck stiff, that they might not hear, nor receive instruction."* Even in these days, when you continue to disobey the Lord; He has told me to instruct you while you are being rebellious. Look at Ezekiel 2:3–5.

> *And he said unto me, Son of man, I send thee to the children of Israel, to a rebellious nation that hath rebelled against me: they and their fathers have transgressed against me, even unto this very day. For they are impudent children and stiffhearted. I do send*

thee unto them; and thou shalt say unto them, Thus saith the Lord God. And they, whether they will hear, or whether they will forbear, (for they are a rebellious house,) yet shall know that there hath been a prophet among them.

Now look at Jeremiah 7:25–27.

Since the day that your fathers came forth out of the land of Egypt unto this day I have even sent unto you all my servants the prophets, daily rising up and sending them:

Yet they hearkened not unto me, nor inclined their ear, but hardened their neck: they did worse than their fathers. Therefore thou shall speak all these words unto them; but they will not hearken to thee; thou shalt also call unto them; but they will not answer thee.

Even in these days the Lord has sent to you his servants the prophets and you still refuse to hear them. But you will heed to the false prophets that God did not send, giving heed to seducing spirits and doctrines of devils. Look at 1 Timothy 4:1–2.

Now the Spirit speaketh, expressly, that in the latter times some shall depart from the faith, giving heed to seducing spirits, and doctrines of devils; Speaking lies in hypocrisy; having their conscience seared with a hot iron.

So the Lord has told me to go along with whatever you choose to do, because you will not hear what I have to say to you, even though it's coming from His word the Bible. For you are not rejecting me, but you are rejecting Him. Look at 1 Samuel 8:7–8.

And the LORD said unto Samuel, Hearken unto the voice of the people in all that they say unto thee: for they have not rejected thee, but they have rejected me, that I should not reign over them. According to all the works which they have done since the day that I brought them up out of Egypt even unto this day, wherewith they have forsaken me, and serve other gods, so do they also unto thee.

Now hear what the LORD says in 1 Corinthians 14:38. "If any man be ignorant, let him be ignorant."

Jeremiah 7:28 says, *"But thou shall say unto them, This is a nation that obeyeth not the voice of the Lord their God, nor receiveth correction: truth is perished, and is cut off from their mouth."* Truly, this whole nation continue to disobey the Lord, and refuse to receive His correction. there is no truth in them, not even in their mouths.

Look at Jeremiah 2:30. *"In vain have I smitten your children: they receive no correction: your own sword hath devoured your prophets, like a destroying lion."* Now look at Jeremiah 5:3. *"O Lord, are not thine eyes upon the truth? thou hast stricken them, but they have not grieved; thou hast consumed them, but they refuse to receive correction; they have made their faces harder than a rock; they have refused to return."*

And now look at Isaiah 1:4–5.

> *Ah sinful nation, a people laden with iniquity, a seed*
> *of evildoers, children that are corrupters; they have*
> *forsaken the* LORD, *they have provoked the Holy one*
> *of Israel unto anger, they are gone away backward.*
> *Why should ye be stricken any more? ye will revolt*
> *more and more: the whole head is sick, and the whole*
> *heart faint."*

People even in these days refuse to listen to the LORD.

Jeremiah 7:29 says, *"Cut off thine hair, O Jerusalem, and cast it*
away, and take up a lamentation on high places; for the Lord hath
rejected and forsaken the generation of his wrath." Cut off your hair
means to pull your hair and become bald, because you are going
into captivity. Look at Micah 1:16. *"Make thee bald, and poll thee*
for thy delicate children; enlarge thy baldness as the eagle; for they
are gone into captivity from thee." And take up a lamentation on
high places, means to call all the mourning women that cry at
funerals. And let them cry for us. Look at Jeremiah 9:17–18.

> *Thus saith the* LORD *of hosts, Consider ye, and call for*
> *the mourning women, that they may come, and send*
> *for cunning women, that they may come; And let them*
> *make haste, and take up a walling for us, that our eyes*
> *may run down with tears, and our eyelids gush out*
> *with waters.*

For why, let us look at the rest of this verse in Jeremiah 7:29.
"For the Lord hath rejected and forsaken the generation of his

wrath." And the Lord is doing this because of Jeremiah 7:30. *"For the children of Judah have done evil in my sight, saith the Lord: they have set their abominations in the house which is called by my name, to pollute it."* Look at Jeremiah 23:11 and Jeremiah 32:34.

For both prophet and priest are profane; yea, in my house have I found their wickedness, saith the LORD (23:11).

But they set their abominations in the house, which is called by my name, to defile it (32:34).

Now everything you have read in Jeremiah 7:1–30, has been written to warn you that you are not right with God, and you need to repent and turn to Him. If you don't you will in no way be caught up when the rapture comes. You will be like the five foolish virgins that took no oil when they went to meet the bridegroom (the Lord Jesus). Look at Matthew 25:1–13.

Then shall the kingdom of heaven be likened unto ten virgins, which took their lamps, and went forth to meet the bridegroom. And five of them were wise, and five were foolish. They that were foolish took their lamps, and took no oil with them: But the wise took oil in their vessels with their lamps. While the bridegroom tarried, they all slumbered and slept. And at midnight there was a cry made, Behold, the bridegroom cometh; go ye out to meet him. Then all those virgins arose, and trimmed their lamps. And the foolish said unto the wise, Give us of your oil; for our lamps are gone out. But the wise answered, saying, Not so; lest there be not enough for us and you: but go ye rather to them that sell, and buy for yourselves. And while they went to buy, the bridegroom came; and they that were ready went in with him to the marriage: and the door was shut.

Afterward came also the other virgins, saying, Lord, Lord, open to us. But he answered and said, Verily I say unto you, I know you not. Watch therefore, for ye know neither the day nor the hour wherein the Son of man cometh.

You see the Lord may come at any time and you must be ready when He does. Look at Matthew 24:44. *"Therefore by ye also ready: for in such an hour as ye think not the Son of man cometh."* Also look at 1 Thessalonians 5:2. *"For yourselves know perfectly that the day of the Lord cometh as a thief in the night."* The oil in this parable is the Holy Spirit.

You all heard from preachers that have not been called, and they tell you that you are still saved. That is not so. Now you were saved when you first called on the Lord Jesus, because it is written in Romans 10:13. Let's look at it. *"For whosoever shall call upon the name of the Lord shall be saved."* But if you have not continued serving Him as you should have, you may have lost your salvation. Let us look at the first parable in Matthew 13:1–9, and you will see what I'm talking about.

The same day went Jesus out of the house, and sat by the sea side. And great multitudes were gathered together unto him, so that he went into a ship, and sat; and the whole multitude stood on the shore. And he spake many things unto them in parables, saying, Behold, a sower went forth to sow; And when he sowed, some seeds fell by the way side, and the fowls came and devoured them up: Some fell upon stony places, where they had not much earth: and forth they sprung up, because they had no deepness of earth: And when the sun was up they were scorched; and because they had no root; they withered away. And some fell among thorns; and the thorns sprung up, and choked them: but other fell into good ground, and brought forth fruit, some an hundredfold, some sixtyfold, some thirtyfold. Who hath ears to hear, let him hear.

The Lord Jesus will explain this parable beginning in verse 18. But let us look at why He is speaking in parables to you. And why you may not still be saved.

Let us look at Matthew 13:10–17.

And the disciples came, and said unto him, Why speakest thou unto them in parables? He answered and said unto them, Because it is given unto you to know the mysteries of the kingdom of heaven, but to them it is not given. For whosoever hath, to him shall be given, and he shall have more abundance: but whosoever hath not, from him shall be taken away even that he hath. Therefore speak I to them in parables: because they seeing see not; and hearing they hear not, neither do they understand. And in them is fulfilled the prophecy of Esaias, which saith, By hearing ye shall hear, and shall not understand; and seeing ye shall see, and shall not perceive: For this people's heart is wax gross, and their heart is dull of hearing, and their eyes they have closed; lest at any time they should see with their eyes, and hear with their ears, and should understand with their heart, and should be converted, and I should heal them. But blessed are your eyes, for they see: and your ears, for they hear. For verily I say unto you, That many prophets and righteous men have desired to see those things which ye see, and have not seen them; and to hear those things which ye hear, and have not heard them."

The prophecy of Isaiah, you will find in Isaiah 6:9–12. Let us look at these scriptures.

And he said, go, and tell this people. Hear ye indeed, but understand not; and see ye indeed, but perceive not. Make the heart of this people fat, and make their ears heavy, and shut their eyes; lest they see with their eyes, and hear with their ears, and understand with their heart, and convert, and be healed. Then said I, Lord, how long? And he answered. Until the cities be wasted without inhabitant, and the houses without men, and the land be utterly desolate, And the LORD have removed men far away, and there be a great forsaking in the midst of the land.

You see that the Lord has closed the eyes, ears, and hearts of those that are lost, so that they cannot understand the gospel. It is hidden from them, because the god of this world (the devil) has blinded them that believe not, but the Lord has given this ministry to them that faint not. Look at 2 Corinthians 4:1–6.

Therefore seeing we have this ministry, as we have received mercy, we faint not; But have renounced the hidden things of dishonesty, not walking in craftiness, nor handling the word of God deceitfully; but by manifestation of the truth commending ourselves to every conscience in the sight of God. But if our gospel be hid, it is hid to them that are lost: In whom the god of this world hath blinded the minds of them which believe not, lest the light of the glorious gospel of Christ, who is the image of God, should shine unto them. For we preach not ourselves, but Christ Jesus the Lord; and ourselves your servants for Jesus sake. For God, who commanded the light to shine out of darkness, hath shined in our hearts, to give the light of the knowledge of the glory of God in the face of Jesus Christ.

Now we see that the devil has blinded the minds of them that believe not.

Now we are going to look at the explanation of this parable given to us by the Lord Jesus himself. Let us look at Matthew 13:18–23.

Hear ye therefore the parable of the sower. When any one heareth the word of the kingdom, and understandeth it not, then cometh the wicked one (the devil), and catcheth away that which was sown in his heart. This is he which received seed by the way side. But he that received the seed into stony places, the same is he that heareth the word, and anon with joy receiveth it; Yet hath he not root in himself, but dureth for a while: for when tribulation or persecution ariseth because of the word, by and by he is offended. He also that received seed among the thorns is he that heareth the word; and the cares of this world, and the deceitfulness of riches, choke the word, and he becometh unfruitful. But he that received seed into the good ground is he that heareth the word, and understandeth it; which also beareth fruit, and bringeth forth, some an hundredfold, some sixty, some thirty.

Now is the Lord Jesus's explanation of this parable. When anyone hears the word of God, and doesn't understand it, then the devil comes and takes away what was sown in his heart. These are them that received seed by the wayside. He that received the seed in stony places, has heard the word, and immediately with joy received it. But because he had not the word in him; when troubles or persecution came because of the word, he was offended. He also that received the seed among the thorns is he that heard the word, and because he is still conformed to this world and not transformed by the renewing of his mind, the deceitfulness of riches choke the word and he becomes unfruitful. Look at Romans 12:2 *"And be not conformed to this world: but be transformed by the renewing of your mind, that ye may prove what is that good, and acceptable, and perfect, will of God."* And also the deceitfulness of riches (came into a lot of money), choked the word, you became unfruitful (stopped spreading the word). But he that received seed into good ground is he that heard the word, and understood it; and also still is bearing fruit and continue to spread God's word, and brought forth some hundredfold, some sixty and some thirty by witnessing.

Now let's not continue to be complacent. For the Lord is ready to come for the rapture of His church. Look at Romans 13:11. *"And that, knowing the time, that now it is high time to awake out of sleep: for now is our salvation nearer than when we believed."* He is going to first begin in the churches, because they are not doing what they are supposed to be doing, by not obeying the gospel of God. Let's look at 1 Peter 4:17. *"For the time is come that judgment must begin at the house of God: and if it first begin at us, what shall the end be of them that obey not the gospel of God?"* Those that are not obeying the gospel of God will not go up in the rapture, but will have to go through the great tribulation, where they will be surely tried for their disobedience. Not many churches are preparing their people to be ready for the rapture, because their leaders are blind and so are the people. Look at Matthew 15:12–14.

Then came his disciples, and said unto him, Knowest thou that the Pharisees were offended, after they heard this saying? But he answered and said, Every plant, which my heavenly Father hath not planted, shall be rooted up. Let them alone: they be blind leaders of the blind. And if the blind lead the blind, both shall fall in the ditch.

Look now at Luke 6:39–40.

And he spake a parable unto them. Can the blind lead the blind? shall they not both fall into the ditch? The disciple is not above his master: but every one that is perfect shall be as his master.

The prophet Amos spoke of these days in Amos 8:11–12.

Behold the days come, saith the Lord GOD, that I will send a famine in the land, not a famine of bread, nor a thirst for water, but of hearing the words of the Lord. And they shall wander from sea to sea, and from the north even to the east, they shall run to and fro to seek the word of the LORD, and shall not find it.

So you better do as John says in 1 John 4:1. "*Beloved, believe not every spirit, but try the spirits whether they are of God: because many false prophets are gone out into the world.*"

God has shown us of His return for the rapture. He has given His disciples all of His signs of His coming. Look at Matthew 24:3–14.

And as he sat upon the mount of Olives, the disciples came unto him privately, saying. Tell us, when shall these things be? and what shall be the sign of thy coming, and of the end of the world. And Jesus answered and said unto them, Take heed that no man deceive you. For many shall come in my name, saying, I am Christ; and shall deceive many. And ye shall hear of wars and rumors of wars; see that ye be not troubled: for all these things must come to pass, but the end is not yet. For nation shall rise against nation, and kingdom against kingdom: and there shall be famines, and pestilences, and earthquakes, in divers places. All these are the beginning of sorrows. Then shall they deliver you up to be afflicted, and shall kill you: and ye shall be hated of all nations for my name's sake. And then shall many be offended, and shall betray one another, and shall hate one another. And many false prophets shall rise, and shall deceive many. And because iniquity shall abound, the love of many shall wax cold. But he that shall endure unto the end, the same shall be saved. And this gospel of the kingdom shall be preached in all the world for a witness unto all nations; and then shall the end come.

You see the Lord has given all of us his disciples the sign of His coming. The first thing He said, was take heed that no man deceive you. Then the rise of kingdoms and nations against one another. And then there shall be famines, and pestilences, and earthquakes in divers (different) places. Then we shall be afflicted and killed and hated of all nations for His name's sake. Then many shall be offended and betray one another and hate one another, because many false prophets shall rise and deceive many. And iniquity (sin) shall abound (shall multiply), and the love of many shall wax (become) cold. But he that shall endure unto the end shall be saved.

Now we know that we are living in the last days. Because many false prophets will rise and deceive many. We are now living in the last times (hours) for the same reason. Look at 1 John 2:18–20.

> *Little children, it is the last time: and as ye have heard that antichrist shall come, even now are there many antichrists; whereby we know that it is the last time. They went out from us, but they were not of us; for if they had been of us, they would no doubt have continued with us: but they went out, that they might be made manifest that they were not all of us. But ye have an unction from the Holy One, and ye know all.*

Now these antichrists (false prophets and Christians) were part of the true church and were made manifest (known) that they were not true Christians, and the Holy Spirit tells us this expressly (clearly) in 1 Timothy 4:1-2.

> *Now the Spirit speaketh expressly, that in the latter times some shall depart from the faith, giving heed to seducing spirits, and doctrines of devils; Speaking lies in hypocrisy; having their conscience seared with a hot iron.*

We now see that pastors and preachers along with the congregations have turned away from sound doctrines, and to seducing spirits and doctrines of devils. This is what the Bible is talking about in 2 Thessalonians 2:1–5. Let's look at it.

> *Now we beseech you, brethren, by the coming of our Lord Jesus Christ, and by our gathering together*

unto him, That ye be not soon shaken in mind, or be troubled, neither by spirit, nor by word, nor by letter as from us, as that the day of Christ is at hand. Let no man deceive you by any means: for that day shall not come, except there come a falling away first, and that man of sin be revealed, the son of perdition; Who opposeth and exalteth himself above all that is called God, or that is worshipped so that he as God sitteth in the temple of God, shewing himself that he is God. Remember ye not, that, when I was yet with you, I told you these things.

There must first come a falling away, and then the antichrist will come. But now he is being held back by the Holy Spirit, who will be taken out of the way, so that he may come. For even now the mystery of iniquity (sin) is already working; for the Holy Spirit is letting it work until He be taken out of the way, and then the antichrist will come. And those that received not the love of the truth, that they might be saved, God will send them strong delusions, that they should believe a lie. Look now at 2 Thessalonians 2:6–12.

And now ye know what witholdeth that he might be revealed in his time. For the mystery of iniquity doth already work: only he who now letteth will let, until he be taken out of the way. And then shall that Wicked be revealed, whom the Lord shall consume with the spirit of his mouth, and shall destroy with the brightness of his coming: Even him, whose coming is after the working of Satan with all power and signs and lying wonders, And with all deceivableness of unrighteousness in them that perish; because they received not the love of the truth, that they might be saved. And for this cause God shall send them strong delusion, that they should believe a lie: That they all might be damned who believed not the truth, but had pleasure in unrighteousness.

If you take notice; the falling away has already started. The percentage of people attending churches and following God has declined a lot. For they truly are having pleasure in unrighteousness, and God is sending them strong delusions, that they should believe a lie.

This is the reason for the perilous times that have come upon the world. Pandemics, loss of jobs, people not having enough food to feed their families, so much killing, and heart break. All of these are a sign of the last days, along with the falling away. Look at 2 Timothy 3:1-7.

This know also, that in the last days perilous times shall come. For men shall be lovers of their own selves, covetous, boasters, proud, blasphemers, disobedient to parents, unthankful, unholy, Without natural affection, trucebreakers, false accusers, incontinent, fierce, despisers of those that are good, Traitors, heady, high-minded, lovers of pleasures more than lovers of God; Having a form of godliness, but denying the power thereof: from such turn away. For of this sort are they which creep into houses, and lead captive silly women laden with sins, led away with divers lusts,

*Ever learning, and never able to come to the knowledge
of the truth.*

Now all of these things are going on in the world right now.
We can see them every day. And it is because the four horsemen
of Revelation have come and are in this world right now. The Lord
has shown it unto me, and my family are witnesses to it.

We can see all these signs by looking at Revelation 6:1–8.

*And I saw when the Lamb opened one of the seals,
and I heard, as it were the noise of thunder, one of
the four beasts saying, Come and see. And I saw, and
behold a white horse: and he that sat on him had a
bow; and a crown was given unto him: and he went
forth conquering, and to conquer. And when he had
opened the second seal, I heard the second beast say,
Come and see. And there went out another horse that
was red: and power was given to him that sat thereon
to take peace from the earth, and that they should kill
one another: and there was given unto him a great
sword. And when he had opened the third seal, I heard
the third beast say, Come and see. And I beheld, and
lo a black horse; and he that sat on him had a pair
of balances in his hand. And I heard a voice in the
midst of the four beasts say, A measure of wheat for a
penny, and three measures of barley for a penny; and
see thou hurt not the oil and the wine. And when he
had opened the fourth seal, I heard the voice of the
fourth beast say, Come and see. And I looked, and
behold a pale horse: and his name that sat on him was*

Death, and Hell followed with him. And power was given unto him over the fourth part of the earth, to kill with sword, and with hunger, and with death, and with the beast of the earth.

Now let us see the explanation the Lord has given me for these verses. But before you read these explanations, please read Revelation chapters 4 and 5, to get an understanding of who the four beasts are. You see the four beasts in Revelation 4:6–11 are four angels that are always in the presence of the Lord God Almighty, and do all His bidding. They are always in the midst of the throne, and round about the throne. They had six wings and are full of eyes within, always giving praise to the Almighty God and they rest not day and night. And when they gave glory to the Lord, the twenty-four elders that sat on twenty-four thrones cast their golden crowns before the throne giving praise also. For the Lord God Almighty created all things even you, and for His pleasure were you created. In Revelation chapter 5, we see that only the Lord Jesus was found worthy to open the seals of the book that was in the hand of the Father that sat on the throne. So, He went and took the book out of the hand of the Father and began to open it.

Now let us look at the explanation of Revelation 6:1-8, when the Lord Jesus opened the first seal. *"I heard, as it were the noise of thunder, one of the four beasts saying, Come and see."* The first beast ask that I come and see the first horse which has been revealed. And I saw him, and he had a bow: filled with arrows of deception. Coming to deceive people into believing a lie and bringing about the great falling away. He also was given a crown, showing that he had great authority from God to lead people astray. For he came conquering (prevailing and subduing) and to conquer (overcoming and getting the victory) over those that do not understand. For in these last days God has sent a famine into the world. Not a famine of hunger or of thirst for water, but of hearing of the words of the Lord. Look at Amos 8:11–12.

> *Behold the days come, saith the Lord God, that I will send a famine in the land, not a famine of bread, nor a thirst for water, but of hearing the words of the LORD: And they shall wander from sea to sea, and from the north even to the east, they shall run to and fro to seek the word of the LORD, and shall not find it.*

Now we are living in the times of the famine of Amos 8:11. "Behold, the days come, saith the Lord God, that I will send a famine in the land, not a famine of bread, nor a thirst for water, but of hearing the words of the LORD."

Now he should not be as it is. For God has sent some, apostles; and some prophets; and some, evangelist' and some, pastors and teachers; for the perfecting of the saints, for the work of the ministry, for the edifying of the body of Christ: and more. Look at Ephesians 4:11–16.

> *And he gave some, apostles; and some, prophets; and some, evangelists; and some, pastors and teachers; for the perfecting of the saints, for the work of the ministry, for the edifying of the body of Christ: Till we all come in the unity of the faith, and of the knowledge of the Son of God, unto a perfect man, unto the measure of*

the stature of the fulness of Christ: That we henceforth be no more children, tossed to and fro, and carried about with every wind of doctrine, by the sleight of men, and cunning craftiness, whereby they lie in wait to deceive;

But speaking the truth in love, may grow up into him in all things, which is the head, even Christ: From whom the whole body fitly joined together and compacted by that which every joint supplieth, according to the effectual working in the measure of every part, maketh increase of the body unto the edifying of itself in love.

Now let us look at the second seal being opened, in Revelation 6:3–4.

And when he had opened the second seal, I heard the second beast say, Come and see. And there went out another horse that was red: and power was given to him that sat thereon to take peace from the earth, and that they should kill one another; and there was given unto him a great sword.

In these last days we can see that there is no more peace in the earth. And we are getting all kinds of leaders trying their best to bring back peace. But their efforts are in vain. Because from the least, even to the greatest, all are given to covetousness (dishonest gain) even from the prophets to the priest, and they all deal falsely. They were not ashamed of what they were doing, nor could they blush, so when the Lord visits them, they will be cast down. Let us look at Jeremiah 6:13–15.

> *For from the least of them even unto the greatest of them every one is given to covetousness; and from the prophet even unto the priest every one dealeth falsely. They have healed also the hurt of the daughter of my people slightly, saying, Peace, peace; when there is no peace. Were they ashamed when they had committed abomination? nay, they were not at all ashamed, neither could they blush; therefore they shall fall among them that fall: at the time that I visit them they shall be cast down, saith the LORD.*

You will find these same words in Jeremiah 8:10–12.

Now let us look at the last part of verse 4—*"And that they should kill one another; and there was given unto him a great sword."* As we watch the news every day, we can see all the killings that are going on in the world. Hit-and-run auto accidents, killing of people by the police, domestic violent killings, drive by killings, killings over drugs, and by animals. These are all signs of the presence of the red horse. This will happen, because people will be offended, and shall betray one another, and hate one another iniquity shall abound, the love of many shall wax cold. Look at Matthew 24:10 and 12.

> *And then shall many be offended, and shall betray one another, and shall hate one another (10).*

And because iniquity shall abound, the love of many shall wax cold (12).

For in these last days perilous times will come. Look at 2 Timothy 3:1. *"This know also, that in the last days perilous times shall come."* Now the last part of this scripture says that he was given a great sword. The sword in these last days is a gun. If you watch the news, every day people are being shot daily in all kinds of foolish situations. This is just letting you know that these are the last days, and that the sword (gun) is the main weapon.

The third seal: Revelation 6:5–6.

And when he had opened the third seal, I heard the third beast say, Come and see. And I beheld, and lo a black horse; and he that sat on him had a pair of balances in his hand. And I heard a voice in the midst of the four beasts say, A measure of wheat for a penny, and three measures of barley for a penny; and see thou hurt not the oil and the wine.

First, "there appeared a black horse, and he that sat on had a pair of balances in his hand." He is bringing famine and pestilence. As you can see in these last days there are a lot of people who have lost their jobs, bringing hunger for food. Also, the world is having a great pandemic. It is in great need for another stimulus check. People are still trying to recover from this situation with little help. The economy is struggling, and food prices are going up. And people are losing their homes and are unable to pay their rent.

Second, "and see thou hurt not the oil and the wine." The price of gas is regulated to go up any time it wants. Even in the midst of a pandemic. There is just so many different kinds of wine and other spirits, bringing pleasure to so many hearts. All because people are lovers of pleasure more that lovers of God. Look at 2 Timothy 3:4: *"lovers of pleasure more that lovers of God."*

The fourth seal: Revelation 6:7–8.

> *And when he had opened the fourth seal, I heard the voice of the fourth beast say, Come and see. And I looked, and behold a pale horse: and his name that sat on him was Death, and Hell followed with him. And power was given unto them over the fourth part of the earth, to kill with the sword, and hunger, and with death, and with the beasts of the earth.*

All four horses have been released. "This fourth horse is called Death, and Hell followed with him." They travel together and are on separate horses. "And power was given unto them over the fourth part of the earth, to kill with the sword, and hunger, and with death, and with the beast of the earth." To kill with the sword (guns) is being done all over the world. All the wars, people killing each other, for any apparent reason. To kill with hunger: Prices are going up at a very high rate. Many families are hungry from the COVID-19 pandemic, and for loss of jobs. To kill with death; many have been killed in these wars, in the pandemic, and from natural causes. And with the beast of the earth; from the dangerous pets that they have, to wild animals, and by domestic animals. If we pay close attention to what is happening, we will see all these things right now. Right now, we are seeing all the signs of the four horsemen are going on, and the next thing that will happen is the rapture.

When the fifth seal is broken, we will see that the rapture has begun. We will see the souls of the Martyrs that were slain for the word of God, and the testimony which they held: under the altar in heaven. And they cried with a loud voice, asking the Lord, when will He judge and avenge them that dwell on the earth? Look at Revelation 6:9–11.

> *And when he had opened the fifth seal, I saw under the altar the souls of them that were slain for the word of God, and for the testimony which they held: And they cried with a loud voice, saying, How long, O Lord, holy and true, dost thou not judge and avenge our blood on them that dwell on the earth? And white robes were given unto every one of them; and it was said unto them, that they should rest yet for a little season, until their fellowservants also and their brethren, that should be killed as they were, should be fulfilled.*

There will be no souls under the altar in heaven until the rapture. For in Job, we see no one is raptured up until the heaven is no more. All that has died will be asleep until then. Look at Job 14:10–12.

> *But man die and wasteth away: yea, man giveth up the ghost, and where is he? As the waters fail from the sea, and the flood decayeth and drieth up:*
> *So man lieth down, and riseth not: till the heavens be no more, they shall not awake, nor be raised out of their sleep."*

Look also at 1 Thessalonians 4:13–16.

> *But I would not have you to be ignorant, brethren, concerning them which are asleep, that ye sorrow not, even as others which have no hope. For if we believe that Jesus died and rose again, even so them also which sleep in Jesus will God bring with him.*
>
> *For this we say unto you by the word of the Lord, that we which are alive and remain unto the coming of the Lord shall not prevent (precede) them which are asleep. For the Lord himself shall descend from heaven with a shout, with the voice of the archangel, and with the trump of God: and the dead in Christ shall rise first.*

Then we that are the Lord's and remain alive on the earth with them, shall be caught up together with them in the clouds, to meet the Lord in the air, and so shall we ever be with the Lord. Look at 1 Thessalonians 4:17–18.

> *Then we which are alive and remain shall be caught up together with them in the clouds, to meet the Lord in the air: and so shall we ever be with the Lord. Wherefore comfort one another with these words.*

So let us comfort one another with these words. For we have this hope, that when he appears, we shall be as he is. Look at 1 John 3:2. *"Beloved, now are we the sons of God, and it doth not yet appear what we shall be: but we know that, when he shall appear, we shall be like him; for we shall see him as he is."*

Now I will show you the signs of the last days that you have not seen. For you believe that every preacher that you listen to is sent of God. On the contrary, they are not. And I'm going to show why I know they are not. The Bible and the Holy Spirit speaks clearly on this subject. In the book of 2 Peter, Peter tells us that there have always been false prophets, even in these days. And they come bringing in destructive heresies privily, even denying the Lord that bought them. And many shall follow their destructive ways, whereas through covetousness, with feigned words, they shall mislead you. Look at 2 Peter 2:1–3.

> *But there were false prophets also among the people, even as there shall be false teachers among you, who privily shall bring in damnable heresies, even denying the Lord that bought them, and bring upon themselves swift destruction. And many shall follow their pernicious ways; by reason of whom the way of truth shall be evil spoken of. And through covetousness shall they with feigned words make merchandise of you: whose judgment now of a long time lingereth not, and their damnation slumbereth not.*

Right now, we are no longer living in the last days, but in the last times (hours). We know by what the Bible shows us in the book of 1 John. It tells us that in these times many will be following false prophets, and no longer following the true teachings of the Bible. So instead of being Christians, they are antichrists, for they do not follow Jesus Christ, but follow the teachings of men. Let's look at 1 John 2:18–19.

Little children, it is the last time: and as ye have heard that antichrist shall come, even now are there many antichrists; whereby we know that it is the last time. They went out from us, but they were not of us; for if they had been of us, they would no doubt have continued with us: but they went out, that they might be made manifest that they were not all of us.

Now we know this because the Holy Spirit tells us clearly, that in the latter times, that some shall depart from the faith. Giving in to seducing spirits, and doctrines of devils. Speaking lies and becoming hypocrites and having no conscience at all. Look at 1 Timothy 4:1–2.

Now the Spirit speaketh expressly, that in the latter times some shall depart from the faith, giving heed to seducing spirits, and doctrines of devils; Speaking lies in hypocrisy; having their conscience seared with a hot iron.

Now we can only be a hypocrite without the Holy Spirit, because when the Holy Spirit comes he will guide you into all truth. Look at what the Lord Jesus says in John 16:13–14.

Howbeit when he, the Spirit of truth, is come, he will guide you into all truth; for he shall not speak of himself, but whatsoever he shall hear, that shall he speak: and he will shew you things to come. He shall glorify me: for he shall receive of mine, and shall shew it unto you.

Now these days have been spoken of by the prophet Amos. For he says that these days will come when God will send a famine in the land. Not a famine for food, nor a famine for water, but of the hearing of the words of the Lord. Look at Amos 8:11–14.

Behold the days come, saith the Lord God, that I will send a famine in the land, not a famine of bread, nor a thirst for water, but of hearing the words of the LORD: And they shall wander from sea to sea, and from the north even to the east, they shall run to and fro to seek the word of the LORD, and shall not find it. In that day shall the fair virgins and young men faint for thirst. They that swear by the sin of Samaria, and say, Thy god, O Dan, liveth; and, The manner of Beer-sheba liveth; even they shall fall, and never rise up again.

You see that they that continue to sin in the manner of Samaria (continuing to disobey God's commandments) and say God liveth shall fall and not rise up again, let us know that Amos is speaking of the end of times.

And now we know that God will always let us know when He is coming. We all will be aware when He is about to do what He has promised to the whole world. He (God) will first warn us by sounding the trumpets to try to prepare us, and will send His prophets to get us ready for the rapture. Let us see what He says in Amos 3:5–8.

Can a bird fall in a snare upon the earth, where no gin is for him? shall one take up a snare from the earth,

*and have taken nothing at all? Shall a trumpet be
blown in the city, and the people not be afraid? shall
there be evil in a city, and the LORD hath not done it?
Surely the Lord GOD will do nothing, but he revealed
his secret unto his servants the prophets. The lion hath
roared, who will not fear? the Lord GOD hath spoken,
who can but prophesy?*

God will certainly prepare prophets to warn the whole world
when He is about to return for the rapture of His church. He will
truly send evil throughout the world to try to turn people back to
Him and at the same time send His prophets to tell everyone what
He is about to do. That is God's reason for calling and sending
me to prepare you for His coming to rapture up His church. Right
now, you are not ready, and must be prepared to go up. Now,
many think or even believe that they are but are not. Look at 1
Corinthians 10:12 "Wherefore let him that thinketh he standeth
take heed lest he fall."

You see God is long-suffering toward us and doesn't want
anyone to perish. But wants all of us to come to repentance.
Look at 2 Peter 3:9. *"The Lord is not slack concerning his promise,
as some men count slackness; but is long-suffering to-usward,
not willing that any should perish, but that all should come to
repentance."* So let us repent and turn to God and be ready for
the rapture and receive all of His promises. So, sanctify The Lord
in your hearts and be ready always to give an answer to every
man that asks you "What is the reason of your hope?" Look at 1
Peter 3:15. *"But sanctify the Lord God in your hearts; and be ready
always to give an answer to every man that asketh you a reason of*

the hope that is in you with meekness and fear." And be also ready for the Lord will come when you are not looking for Him. Look at Matthew 24:44. *"Therefore be ye also ready; for in such an hour as ye think not the Son of man cometh"* So be thou always ready.

CONCLUSION

Here's all you have to do in order to enter God's rapture. For you believe that you are ready to go up in the rapture, but you are not, and here's why. The Lord says there is none, none that's righteous. None that understandeth. And they are all gone out of the way. They have together become unprofitable. There's none that doeth good. No, not one.

Now, read that again in Romans 3:10–12.

> *As it is written, There is none righteous. No, not one: There is none that understandeth. There is none that seeketh after God.*
>
> *They are all gone out of the way, they are together become unprofitable; There is none that doeth good, no, not one.*

So, everybody thinks they can go to God by their wicked ways or the unrighteous man with his thoughts.

> *Let the wicked forsake his way, and the unrighteous man his thoughts: and let him return unto the Lord, and he will have mercy upon him: and to our God, for He will abundantly pardon. For my thoughts are not your thoughts, and neither are your ways my ways, saith the Lord. For as the heavens are higher than the earth, so are my ways higher than your ways, and my thoughts than your thoughts"* (Isaiah 55:7–9).

Remember in Jeremiah chapter 7 that God tells you to amend your ways and your doings, becoming closer to God and not drifting farther apart. You must be doing the things that He's telling you to do in the Bible to get ready for the rapture, not the things that you wickedly think of, for instance, like getting closer to God by fasting or starving yourself. But do it by His word. Amend your ways and your doings as it is written in Jeremiah 7:3: *"Thus, saith the Lord of hosts, the God of Israel, Amend your ways and your doings, and I will cause you to dwell in this place. And, trust not in lying words."* In other words, let him return unto the Lord, which means to repent. Realize that you truly are a sinner, and you need to repent.

For God says you are backsliding. And He says in Jeremiah 3:12, *"Return, thou backsliding Israel, saith the Lord; and I will not cause mine anger to fall upon you: for I am merciful, saith the Lord…"* And He is very merciful. And He says, "and I will not keep anger forever" But as long as you are backsliding, He is very angry and waiting for you to repent. And He is longsuffering to us, not willing that anyone should perish but that all should come to repentance.

Let's read this again in 2 Peter 3:9. As it is written, *"The Lord is not slack concerning His promise as some men count slackness. But is longsuffering to usward; not willing that anyone should perish, but that all should come to repentance."* So truly admit that you are a sinner. Stop turning away from God by backsliding and repent.

And here's what he says about that in Jeremiah 3:12–15. As it is written,

> *Go and proclaim these words toward the north and say, Return, thou backsliding Israel, saith the Lord;*

and I will not cause mine anger to fall upon you: for I am merciful, saith the Lord and I will not keep anger for ever. Only acknowledge thine iniquity, that thou hast transgressed against the Lord thy God, and hast scattered thy ways to the strangers under every green tree, and ye have not obeyed my voice, saith the Lord.

Turn, O backsliding children, saith the Lord; for I am married unto you: and I will take you one of a city, and two of a family, and I will bring you to Zion: (which is Heaven,) and I will give you pastors according to mine heart, which shall feed you with knowledge and understanding.

You see, the Lord says He's even willing to send somebody to tell you how you should do this: pastors according to His heart. Not the ones that you think are really preachers. Remember what I said about these lying words? God did not send those preachers. So, you must, first of all, truly acknowledge that you are a sinner. Stop turning your back to God, and turn toward him and repent, and He will surely do all of these things. Because God is so merciful and longsuffering. He wishes that none should perish but that all should come to repentance.

Now, after you have repented and turned back to God, stop backsliding. And this is what He says. Jeremiah 29:12–13, as it is written,

Then shall you call upon me and you shall go and pray unto me, and I will harken unto you. And you will seek me and find me when you shall search for me with all your heart.

77

"I will harken unto you" means "I will hear you."

Let's add to all this what God says in Matthew 6:33: "*But, seek ye first the kingdom of God and His righteousness and all these things will be added unto you.*" So, you must seek God every day, all the time. And no matter what you ask of Him it shall be given unto you. Because this is what he wants of you; He wants people to worship Him.

So read His word at least three times every day so that you may learn and begin to keep his commandments. That is a very important roll, because without knowing God's commandments, it shows that you do not love Him.

Start at Genesis and continue throughout the Bible and go all the way through the book of Revelation. And then start all over again and read from Genesis through Revelation.

And the next thing you should do is pray. The Bible tells you to pray without ceasing. You will find this in the first book of Thessalonians 5:17: "*Pray without ceasing.*"

Now listen to James 5:16: "*Confess your faults one to another and pray one for another that you may be healed. The effectual fervent prayer of a righteous man availeth much.*"

You will find this scripture in Luke 18:1. "*And he spake a parable unto them to this end; that men are to always pray and not faint.*" Now let's hear these words in Psalm 55:16-17: "*As for me, I will call upon God and the Lord shall save me. Evening, morning and at noon will I pray and cry aloud and He shall hear my voice.*"

Now, after you have begun reading the word and have read it as instructed (from Genesis to Revelation), the one thing I truly ask is that you not try even to understand it. Because when you begin all over again in the book of Genesis, the Holy Spirit will begin to start taking over. And He will begin to show you things in the Bible, and maybe you'll get a better understanding and start keeping God's commandment, everything that you read. And please don't forget while you are reading His word to pray. Pray always without ceasing. Because the effectual, fervent prayer of a righteous man availeth much. Men are to always pray and not cease. And when you pray, pray in the way that God showed His disciples to pray. First of all, pray according to the words that are in Matthew 6:9-15. And also as it is written in Luke 11:1–4.

And it came to pass, that, as he was praying in a certain place, when he ceased, one of his disciples asked him, Lord, teach us to pray as John also taught his disciples. And He said unto them, When ye pray, say, Our Father which art in heaven, Hallowed be thy name, Thy kingdom come. Thy will be done, as in heaven, so in earth. Give us this day our daily bread. And forgive us our sins; for we also forgive every one that is indebted to us. And lead us not into temptation; but deliver us from evil.

There's one other thing that's very important to trying to get into the rapture. And it is receiving the Holy Spirit. You all believe that you can "catch" the Holy Spirit by attending church on Sundays, that you catch Him on Sunday and then He leaves on Monday. That is not so. Here's how you keep the Holy Spirit. You've been reading, learning God's commandments. And then you started praying without ceasing. And you have learned His commandments. Now here's what you have to do: start keeping God's commandments, and it will show you that you really love

Him. Because now you are starting to hear His voice and to do as it says.

Listen to the words of the Lord Jesus Christ in John 14:15-16. Now, listen to these words.

If you love me, keep my commandments.
And I will pray the Father and He will send
you another comforter. That He may abide with you
forever.

Look again in verse 16 in the last few words. He will abide with you forever. That means the Holy Spirit, once He comes, He will never leave you unless you do something really foolish, and God takes Him away from you. Verse 17 continues, *"Even the Spirit of truth; whom the world cannot receive, because it seeth him not, neither knoweth him: but ye know him; for he dwelleth with you, and shall be in you. I will not leave you comfortless: I will come to you."* Once you receive the Holy Spirit, he will never ever leave you. So, he will be always with you as a comforter until the Lord Jesus Christ comes back to receive you into Heaven.

Here are more things about the Holy Spirit. Look at John 14:21. As it is written, *"He that hath my commandments and keepeth them, he it is that loveth me: and he that loveth me shall be loved of my Father, and I will love him, and will manifest myself to him."*

And verse 23 says, *"Jesus answered and said unto him, If a man love me, he will keep my words: and my father will love him, and we will come unto him, and make our abode with him."*

Verse 26 continues. *"But the Comforter, which is the Holy Ghost, whom the Father will send in my name, he shall teach you all things, and bring all things to your remembrance, whatsoever*

I have said unto you." The Holy Spirit will come and teach you everything you have read and prayed about in the Bible. And teach you all things.

There's nothing, if you continue to read and pray, that He will not give you. Because it all comes from the Lord Jesus Christ. It's all His word. Because, if y'all remember, in the book of John 17:17, the Lord Jesus Christ said, *"Thy word is truth,"* when He was praying to the Father.

John 15:26 states, *"But when the Comforter is come, whom I will send unto you from the Father, even the Spirit of truth which proceedeth from the father, he shall testify of me:"* He shall testify of the Lord Jesus Christ because He's come to speak only the word of God to you and nothing else.

Now remember these things. Once you receive Him, He will never leave you. He will be with you forever. He is sent to you by the Father with prayers from the Lord Jesus Christ. And He's come to teach you everything that you need in order to enter the kingdom of God. He is your teacher; and He will teach you all that the Lord Jesus Christ has gotten from the Father and has put in the Bible.

Now, you must receive everything that you've just been taught to receive the Holy Spirit. Because it is very important that you have him. Because, right now, I'm going to tell you something that you probably didn't know. But it's in the Bible, so it's true, and you should know.

Without the Holy Spirit, you do not have the Lord Jesus Christ!

Now, we are truly going to look at this. In the book of Romans 8:9. Listen to these words as it is written: *"But you are not in the flesh but in the spirit, if so be that the Spirit of God dwell in you.*

Now if any man have not the Spirit of Christ, he is none of his." So, in order to be truly saved you must also have the blessed Holy Spirit. And, of course, you know that you really need the Lord Jesus Christ to get to the Father. Because, He says it strictly in John 14:6. *"Jesus says unto him, I am the way, the truth, and the life: No man cometh unto the father but by me."* So, now you know you need the blessed Holy Spirit in order to have the Lord Jesus Christ. And you need the Lord Jesus Christ because He is the only way you can come unto the Father. It's only by Him.

BIBLE VERSE EXPLANATIONS

Ezekiel 2:4
impudent= stubborn

Ezekiel 2:5
forbear = refuse

Isaiah 6:10
healed = saved

Hebrews 13:7
conversation = lifestyle

Psalm 19:7
law of the Lord = the word
testimony of the Lord = the word

Romans 8:26
Spirit = Holy Spirit
infirmities = weaknesses

Romans 8:27
he that searches the hearts = The Lord Jesus

John 14:16
Comforter = The Holy Spirit

Romans 8:9
his = The Lord Jesus

John 16:14
me - The Lord Jesus

Galatians 5:17
lusteth = desires what is
contrary = opposite

Galatians 5:19
lasciviousness = filthiness

Galatians 5:20
idolatry = image worship
variance = strife
sedition = division
heresies = disunion

Galatians 5:21
revellings = rioting

Galatians 5:26
vain = empty

James 3:17
intreated = be in compliance

Romans 8:11
quicken = make alive

Romans 8:13
mortify = put to death

Ezekiel 9:2
One man among them = the Holy Spirit

Ephesians 4:1
vocation = calling

Ephesians 4:19
lasciviousness = lustful desires

Ephesians 2:3
conversation = lifestyle

Ephesians 2:5
quickened = made us alive
quickened us together in Christ = by grace ye are saved

Ephesians 5:10
circumspectly = carefully

I Thessalonians 4:5
concupiscence =passion of lust

2 Peter 2:1
damnable = destructive
heresies = destructive evil

2 Peter 2:2
pernicious = damnable

2 Peter 2:3
covetousness = fraud

feigned = fictitious
merchandise = buy and sell/mislead

1 John 2:18
last time = last hour
manifest = declared

1 John 2:20
unction = anointing

1 John 4:1
try=test

1 Timothy 4:1
Spirit = Holy Spirit
expressly = clearly

Matthew 23:13
suffer = allow

23:15
proselyte = convert

Matthew 23:27
sepulchers = tombs

Jude 1:8
dignities = higher powers

Jeremiah 7:15
works = wickedness and abominations

Jeremiah 7:19
confusion of their own faces = shame and destruction

Isaiah 1:13
vain oblations = useless gifts

Ezekiel 2:5
forbear = not listen

Matthew 13:20
anon = immediately

Matthew 15:12
Pharisees = preachers and teachers

2 Thessalonians 2:3
that man of sin = the antichrist

2 Timothy 3:2
covetous = greedy

Revelation 6:1
the Lamb = Jesus Christ

Jeremiah 6:13
covetousness = dishonest gain

Matthew 24:12
iniquity = sin
abound = increase
wax = grow

2 Timothy 3:1
perilous = fierce

John 16:13
the Spirit of truth = Holy Spirit

Amos 8:11
bread = food

Amos 3:5
gin = trap

John 15:26
Comforter = Holy Spirit
Spirit of truth = Holy Spirit

Printed in the United States
by Baker & Taylor Publisher Services